GENERAL ROBERT E. LEE

THE SOUTH'S PEERLESS SOLDIER AND LEADER

By CAPTAIN SAMUEL A. ASHE

REPRINTED BY

Wake Forest, NC
www.scuppernongpress.com

General Robert E. Lee
The South's Peerless Soldier And Leader
By Captain Samuel A. Ashe

Edited by Frank B. Powell, III

©2014 The Scuppernong Press

First Printing

The Scuppernong Press
PO Box 1724
Wake Forest, NC 27588
www.scuppernongpress.com

Cover and book design by Frank B. Powell, III

All rights reserved

Printed in the United States of America

No part of this book may be reproduced or transmitted in any form or by any means, electronic or mechanical, including photocopying, recording, or by any information and storage and retrieval system, without written permission from the editor and/or publisher.

International Standard Book Number
                                ISBN 978-0-9898399-8-3

Library of Congress Control Number: 2014954348

Contents

Introduction ----------------------------------- *iii*

A Heroic Leader ---------------------------------- 1

Captain Ashe's Address --------------------------- 3

The Crosses of Honor ---------------------------22

The Rear Guard ---------------------------------- 24

About the Author--------------------------------27

Introduction

What a night it must have been! You can almost see it in your mind's eye — a dimly lit room in the North Carolina State Capitol packed with Confederate Veterans, members of the United Daughters of the Confederacy, state and local dignitaries along with members of the general public — the smell of smoke and flickering light from the four fireplaces in the House Chamber.

Confederate Flags were hanging everywhere, including some which had flown on the battlefields of the War for Southern Independence carried by North Carolina soldiers. Portraits of General Robert E. Lee, Zebulon Vance and George Washington silently observed the proceedings.

January 20, 1904, was a Wednesday, the day after General Robert E. Lee's ninety-seventh birthday. All of these people had gathered to honor this event and the man most regarded, as not only the greatest Southerner, but the greatest American who had ever lived. This tradition continues in the twenty-first century and this editor hopes it continues for many centuries to come.

However, it will be up to future generations to continue to honor, not only General Robert E. Lee, but all Confederate Veterans. The original pamphlet has been out of print for more than a hundred years and not many were printed or survive today. That is the purpose of reprinting this small book. Not only to honor General Lee and Captain Ashe, but all Confederate Veterans and to leave this information for future generations.

— Frank B. Powell, Editor

ORATION

GEN'L ROBERT E. LEE

THE SOUTH'S PEERLESS SOLDIER AND LEADER

By CAPTAIN SAMUEL A. ASHE

RALEIGH, N.C., JAN. 20, 1904

JOHNSON PETTIGREW CHAPTER, U.D.C.
RALEIGH, N.C.

RALEIGH:

W. S. SHERMAN & CO., PRINTERS AND BINDERS

1906

General Robert E. Lee — Captain Samuel A. Ashe

A HEROIC LEADER

Tribute from the loving heart of the South was given last night in memory of its peerless soldier-leader when men and women, representatives of Raleigh's best life, thronged the hall of the House of Representatives at the exercises held in celebration of the anniversary of the birth of General Robert E. Lee. It was a goodly assemblage, and it was devout in its intentness. The music, the oration, the prayer, the poem and the presentation of the Crosses of Honor, all were typical of the South, which symbolized, in this tribute to Lee, its love and veneration of all who wore the grey. The applause that greeted each event of the evening was fraught with patriotism.

Confederate colors were there in abundance. Back of the speaker's desk a great Confederate flag was hung, flanked by smaller Stars and Bars, one of which was tattered and torn from shells in a deadly conflict, and another the flag of the L. O'B. Branch Camp. In front of the desk was a large steel engraving of General Lee on horseback, and this was adorned with tiny Confederate flags.

The meeting was presided over by Adjutant J.C. Birdsong, of the L. O'B. Branch Camp, in the absence of Commander Stronach. Seated with the orator of the evening, Captain S. A. Ashe, was also Rev. M. M. Marshall, the chaplain of the occasion. On one side was ranged the band of the Blind Institution, which rendered patriotic music during the evening. From the left the loving eyes of Vance looked down from his counterfeit presentment, while from the other canvas the pictured form of the "Father of His Country" added dignity to the impressive scene, gazed upon by veterans grey, by mothers who had borne war's privations at home, by sons and daughters, and by grandsons and granddaughters, whose hearts all have within them the fires of undying devotion to the South, and love for the heroes who offered life as a libation in its defense.

The audience had been ushered to places by four gallant little gentlemen, whose insignia of red and white told that they were the marshals of the evening, these being Masters George Ashe, Leo Heartt, Jessie Primrose and Robert Waitt.

Following the music which began the exercises, Adjutant Birdsong presented Rev. M. M. Marshall, who led in prayer. In his petition he thanked God for the life of His servant, General Lee, who had been faithful even unto death. He alluded to his self-sacrificing life, and prayed that it might ever prove an inspiration to the youth of the land to noble deeds. The audience joined with him in one voice in the Lord's Prayer.

Adjutant Birdsong, who, in Company B, Twelfth Regiment of Virginia Infantry, had seen service, next spoke of the unexpected honor he had in acting as master of ceremonies, and that while it was a duty, such was never onerous when demanded by the Daughters of the Confederacy, this graceful tribute being paid to the members of the Johnston-Pettigrew Chapter, under whose auspices the celebration was held, and who were present in large numbers. He told of the deathless love of the Confederate soldier for General Lee, and declared that though dead he lived in the hearts of every veteran and every woman of the South. In felicitous terms he introduced Captain Ashe, who delivered the oration of the evening.

Captain Ashe's Address

It was an address full of love to Lee, abounding in historic facts telling of the days of the war, and the words were fitting words, coming from a Confederate, who was a member of Company I, Eighteenth Regiment, and had served on the general staff. Many times was Captain Ashe applauded, and applause greeted the close of his able and valuable address.

Necessarily our report of the address is much curtailed. It was an elaborate presentation of the character of Lee, and a graphic account of his military career, giving the details of his famous campaigns that won for him imperishable fame. Among other things Captain Ashe said:

Lord Wolsely discussing Napoleon says that extraordinary man took Caesar as his military model, and even modeled his stirring addresses to his soldiers after Cae sar, but, with true English antipathy to this product of the French Revolution, he adds with withering sarcasm, "that Caesar was a gentleman." Yea, verily, that blue-eyed, round-faced, curly-headed Roman, whose fame as an orator, historian and warrior resounds through the corridors of time, was a gentleman; and if Ovid is to be believed, his body was borne beyond the clouds to the serene heavens, where he became an associate of the Roman Deities.

In our time, the greatest and most glorious soldier of modern ages also was a gentleman — and we embalm the memory of his virtues on the altars of our hearts, and hold him almost worthy of our love and veneration.

President Tyler mentions that among the early emigrants who landed at Jamestown, there were thirty-four noblemen of the most ancient families of the English peerage, and 128 knights baronets. It is this class of country gentlemen that has furnished the most brilliant characters in the splendid galaxy of eminent men who have adorned the annals of Great Britain. In Virginia, these high-bred gentry spread themselves throughout the tidewater region, and their descendants have won for the Old Dominion the proud distinction of being the mother of States and of statesmen. Particularly has the small county of Westmoreland, lying between the Rappahannock and the Potomac, been the matrix of great characters. There, in the opening years of the nineteenth century, could be seen a lovely matron, the mistress of an elegant mansion, surrounded by luxury, and the center of a refined and noble connection. She, herself, could trace her lineage back through many heroes to Robert Bruce, the patriot of Scotland, while her husband, also of honorable lineage, had won fame and high honors in the war for independence, and as Light Horse Harry, had left his impress on the history of his country.

But men follow the mother rather than the father. Seldom has a great, strong man been born to a weak woman. By nature, our heritage is largely from the female side, and the children of Annie Hill Carter, the wife of Light Horse Harry Lee, had their hearts ennobled by the rich blood of Robert, the Bruce. Nurtured under her influence, living in an atmosphere where only virtues could flourish, her children naturally developed into exemplary characters.

To the interested and anxious household that gathered at Stratford this night, ninety-seven years ago, there came a child, destined, like Caesar, to fill the measure of fame as a soldier and a gentleman.

A few miles distant, on the same noble Potomac, in the same neighborhood, Washington had been born; now it was Robert Edward Lee, in many respects the peer, in some the superior, of the great patriot — whose untimely death was still freshly mourned by the people, and the eulogy of the orator, Richard Henry Lee, still reverberated throughout the continent: "First in war, first in peace, and first in the hearts of his countrymen."

Hardly had Washington passed away at Mt. Vernon before Lee was born at Stratford.

When Robert Lee was four years of age, his parents moved into the neighboring town of Alexandria; and three years later his father departed for a long sojourn in the West Indies, from which he never returned. So, during his boyhood days, Robert Lee was under the sole care of, his mother, the home-life being so affectionate and tender as to excite our interest and awaken our sympathy. An elder sister had fallen into ill health; and Mrs. Lee herself was an invalid. So situated, Robert became both a daughter and a son to his mother. Under her direction, he was housekeeper of his home. His spare moments were spent at her side. He was her nurse and daily companion — read to her, rode with her and comforted her. He grew to resemble her in disposition, in gentle manners, in careful thought. Duty became the watchword of his life. Duty to his Maker, duty to his home, and duty in that station of life in which it had pleased God to place him.

A visit to President Andrew Jackson obtained his appointment to the military academy at West Point, where his fine bearing gained for him the front rank in the student body. It was while a cadet, in the glory of his flashing brass buttons, that he first met the light of the household of Arlington, Mary Custis, whose mother was a step-daughter of Washington. On graduating, he began his first campaign to win the noblest prize that man can seek, the heart of a beloved woman. The modest public notice of the marriage was in keeping with the idea of the times: "Married, June 30, 1831, at Arlington House, by Rev. Mr. Keith, Lieutenant Robert E. Lee, of the United States Corps of Engineers, to Miss Mary A. R. Custis, only daughter of G. W. P. Custis, Esq."

Princes and princesses, born to the purple, might have well envied their condition in life. In the circumstances that make exalted station they were among the first in the whole of the New World; while the bride was rich in graces and her husband had capacity, character and excellence, and a gentle bearing that distinguished him above other men.

In seven years he had attained the rank of captain, and when, in 1845, war opened with Mexico, he was assigned to the first army of invasion, under General Wool. While man is born to wedlock and it is his natural portion in life, still it modifies his entire existence. The longings of the ambitious young officer, amid the mountains of Mexico, were for the smiles of his wife, and thoughts of home were mingled with the anxieties of his situation. Despite his strenuous duties, his great heart turned to the object of his love on the banks of the Potomac.

From Saletto, on Christmas, 1846, after the excitement of an apprehended attack that had disturbed their Christmas dinner, he wrote to his wife: "Finding that the enemy did not come, preparations were again made for dinner. We have had many happy Christmasses together. It is the first time that we have been entirely separated at this holy time since our marriage. I trust that this is the last time I shall be absent from you during life."

With Wool he rendered conspicuous service, so that when Scott arrived, that general particularly asked that Lee might be sent to him, and he became the military adviser of the commander-in-chief.

He who had been a mother's boy, who had learned to practice watchfulness and carefulness amid the solicitude of the sick-room, now was to reap a rich reward for his habitual painstaking and regard for details, for his devotion to duty and self-sacrifice.

The responsibilities of an engineer officer in a strange country, amid mountains and impracticable roads, and in the face of a numerous foe, are very great. He must determine what points should be occupied, and whether or not it is practicable to reach them, and to hold them against the assaults of the enemy; he must outline the battle, and sketch the plan of the campaign. It so happened that even more than this devolved on Captain Lee. In that unknown and difficult region, he had himself to become the active scout to gain needed information. In this work, no task was too arduous, no endurance beyond his powers, no undertaking too perilous for him to perform it. To say that he displayed fine military genius; to say that he repeatedly won high distinction by gallant conduct, that he made reputation as an engineer by his courage and devotion, conveys no adequate idea of the result of his splendid services.

Daily the imminent occasion called for some extraordinary feat, and daily Lee rose equal to the emergency, and won applause by his admirable conduct.

At one time, with Wool, after a night scout to locate the enemy, during which, with only one unwilling

Mexican guide, he had ridden at a gallop forty miles, and gained a clue to the enemy's location, after only three hours rest, he was again in the saddle, and piloted a body of cavalry still further to find the Mexican encampment. His endurance was wonderful. His career was a steady blaze of glory. The siege of Cerro Gordo brought him promotion; so also Cherubusco, while Chaupultapec gained him the brevet rank of Colonel — the highest in the Corps of Engineers.

A simple narrative of his life is his best eulogium. So let me detain you with a brief account of a single incident. Near Cherubusco, the route of the army struck a triangular region of volcanic scoria, called the Pedregal. It was a wild waste — a vast surface of volcanic rocks, a sea of congealed lava, broken into every conceivable form by sharp ridges and deep fissures. It was pathless and precipitous, requiring the explorer to spring from rock to rock, often so sharp that only one foot could gain foothold on them. To strike the enemy's flank, Lee conducted a body of troops across that difficult region. They went as stragglers — every man for himself; but eventually before nightfall, one by one, they had reached the further side. At night, a council of war was held by the officers. Lee's suggestion for the attack was adopted, and he hastened to set out on his return to advise General Scott of the proposed movement. But a fierce storm had set in. The rain was falling in torrents, and the darkness was intense. Lee left the council, and his way lightened only by the lurid flashes of the electric storm, began the perilous journey across that rocky chaos; scarcely a step of the whole route could have been taken without risk of instant death. Anxious for information, General Scott had sent forward seven different officers to cross the Pedregal, but every one had returned, finding it impossible to cross. Not one succeeded in getting through. But Lee succeeded. At midnight, he reached Scott's headquarters safe. General Scott afterwards bore this testimony: "That Captain Lee's night crossing of the Pedregal, alone in that terrific storm, was the greatest feat of physical and moral courage performed by any individual in my knowledge, pervading the entire campaign in Mexico."

By three o'clock the next morning, Lee was conducting an assaulting column through darkness and rain to an eminence in the rear of the Mexican position — and at sunrise, the battle was won.

Every day made some new demand on Lee's skill, daring and courage, and every day he measured up higher and higher as a competent soldier. General Scott, who won imperishable honors by his constant victories, did not hesitate to ascribe his success, in large part, to the skill, valor and undaunted energy of Robert E. Lee. And the other officers were of the same opinion. By common consent, Lee wore his honors worthily. All sang his praises. General Wilcox caps his laudation with the following remark: "And then I was much impressed with his fine appearance both on horseback and on foot. He was the handsomest man in the army."

But during all this arduous service, amid all this peril, the heart of the handsomest man in the army was with his home on the banks of the Potomac. As soon as peace came, he hastened to Arlington — from where he wrote to his brother, Captain Sidney Lee, of the navy, the day after his arrival: "Here I am again, perfectly surrounded by Mary and her precious children, who seem to devote themselves to staring at the furrows in my face, and the white hairs in my head." And, continuing in a most affectionate way, he urges his brother "to bring 'Sis' Nan' and all the little ones to see him."

Yes, affection had its home in his heart, and the glory of his brilliant career only made him the more tender and loving to his dear ones. The furrows were on his cheeks, and his hair was whitened — these attested the hard service he had performed; but he received the rich reward of superb capabilities in treasured laudations.

In Mexico with him were Grant, Meade, McClellan, McDowell, Thomas, Hooker, Burnside, Sedgewick, Hancock, Smith, Pillow, Sidney Johnston, Joe Johnston, Bragg, Longstreet, McGruder, Early, A. P. Hill, D. H. Hill, and other companions in arms — all winning honors, some achieving high distinction — but none gathering the splendid laurels that adorned the brow of Robert E. Lee.

Lee was now entering into the maturity of his fine powers. He had never departed from the precepts he had learned at his mother's knee, and had not weakened his constitution by excesses or dissipation. He had always been fond of society, was agreeable in his manners and charming in his conversation, but his sense of duty towards God and man was a potent force that gave to his character an elevation which distinguished him among the officers of the army.

At New York he was a vestryman of the church he attended, and all through life he made public profession of the Christian faith, and of his dependence upon the deity. From the frontier he wrote to his wife: "This is Easter Sunday. I hope you have been able to attend the services at church. My own have been performed alone in my tent — I hope, with an humble, grateful and penitent heart, and will be acceptable to our Heavenly Father. May He continue His mercies to us both, and to all our children, relatives and friends, and in His own good time unite us in His worship, if not on earth, forever in heaven."

Such was the keynote of his life — an humble dependence on the Supreme Being, an abiding faith in the Christian religion, accepting all its mysteries without question, making it the light and beacon to guide his footsteps, and looking with hope to its promises of life everlasting.

While at his distant post, unbending from his cares, his letters home abounded in playfulness, especially those to his little daughter, while sometimes he mingled in his affectionate letters to his wife, a little philosophy. "Systematically pursue," he wrote her; "the best course to recover your lost health. I pray and trust your efforts and the prayers of those who love you, may be favorably answered. Do not worry yourself about things you can't help; but be content to do what you can for the well-being of what properly belongs to you. Commit the rest to those who are responsible, and though it is the part of benevolence to aid all we can, and sympathize with all those who are in need, it is the part of wisdom to attend to our own affairs. Lay nothing too much to heart. Desire nothing too eagerly; nor think that all things can be perfectly accomplished according to our own notions." Army and Navy officers, generally, were not members of any political party. They served their country, and left the civil administration to their countrymen; but necessarily, on the great matters of slavery and secession, Col. Lee had well considered views. On Christmas, 1856, he wrote to his wife: "In this enlightened age there are few, I believe, but will acknowledge that slavery as an institution is a moral and political evil in any country. It is useless to expatiate on its disadvantages. I think it, however, a greater evil to the white man than to the black race; and while my feelings are strongly interested in behalf of the latter, my sympathies are stronger for the former. The blacks are immeasurably better off here than in Africa, morally, socially and physically. The painful discipline they are undergoing is necessary for their instruction as a race, and I hope will prepare and lead them to better things. How long their subjections may be necessary is known and ordered by a wise and merciful Providence. Their emancipation will sooner result from a mild and melting influence than the storms and contests of fiery controversy. This influence, though slow, is sure. While we see the course of the final abolition of slavery is onward, and we give it the aid of our prayers and all justifiable means in our power, we must leave the progress as well as the result in God's hands. Is it not strange that the descendants of those Pilgrim Fathers, who crossed the Atlantic to preserve the freedom of their opinion, have always proved themselves intolerant of the spiritual liberty of others?"

Acting on his own notions of what was right and best, Lee had freed his own slaves, and Mr. Curtis in his will in 1857, provided that the slaves Mrs. Lee would have inherited with the Arlington estate, should after five years likewise be emancipated. Thus neither Lee nor his wife was pecuniarily interested in the perpetuation of slavery at the South; and they had given to the world the highest evidence of their antislavery views by setting their own slaves free.

On the question of secession, Colonel Lee doubtless entertained the view that it was lawful, and within the province of the States; although personally, he was opposed to the movement and deprecated war. When Lee was a cadet at West Point, one of the text-books used there was a treatise on the Constitution, written by Rawle, an eminent lawyer of Philadelphia, in which the right of secession was taught as an acknowledged constitutional right. The right was claimed by New England statesmen when Lee was a boy; was openly asserted in 1820, was re-asserted by Calhoun, and admitted by many in 1833, and it was held as a principle by many of the most eminent characters of the country. Still, Lee loved the Union and the flag, and apprehended that war would follow secession, and he did not favor it. The Union was largely the work of Washington, and Lee hoped that it might be perpetuated. In January, 1861, he wrote to his wife that "he could not anticipate any greater calamity for the country than the dissolution of the Union, and that he was willing to sacrifice everything but honor for its preservation."

Toward the end of February, 1861, Colonel Lee was summoned to Washington by General Scott, and reached there on March 1st, three days before Mr. Lincoln was inaugurated. All public matters were now in a whirlpool of chaos.

The right of self-government, claimed by a dozen great American commonwealths, and involving the independence of ten millions of people, was denied.

Conceived in sin and brought forth in iniquity, actual war had been begun by a breach of faith on the part of the malignant Republicans. And with great adroitness they combined to fire the Northern heart and solidify the North in the support of their designs. On the 15th of April, President Lincoln called for 75,000 men to begin the work of drenching America with blood. Two days later Virginia seceded. The next day Mr. F. P. Blair came to Lee from President Lincoln and offered him command of the Federal army. The following is a statement of Mr. Blair: "I said, I come to you on the part of President Lincoln to ask whether any inducement that we can offer will prevail on you to take command of the Union army." Colonel Lee replied: "If I owned the 4,000,000 slaves, I would cheerfully sacrifice them to the preservation of the Union; but to lift my hand against my own State and people is impossible."

Directly after that offer and refusal, Colonel Lee went to General Scott and told him of it, and then the next day he sent in his resignation.

While Colonel Lee still hoped that war might be averted, yet he was a Virginian, and he felt it incumbent on him to obey the authority of his State, and to cast his fortunes for weal or woe with his people. Two days after he had resigned, Virginia, then having withdrawn from the Union, the Governor of that State invited Lee to Richmond; and he at once proceeded to that city. The Legislature was in session and conferred on him the appointment of Major-General, and invested him with the command of all the forces of that State. He accepted the commission, and entered the military service of Virginia as an independent and sovereign State.

✶ ✶ ✶ ✶ ✶ ✶

It was during the repose after the easy defeat of Burnside's assault, when the Confederate hopes were in an ecstasy of pride and confidence, that the day arrived, when under Mr. Custis's will, the slaves of Mrs. Lee's estate were to be emancipated. General Lee turned aside from his military cares and duties to prepare and execute the deeds of emancipation, and arranged for the future comfort and welfare of the hundred slaves that "would otherwise have been the property of his wife, and that at a time, too, when their home at Arlington had been seized by the Federal Government, and their property there confiscated.

General Lee's life in camp was simple and unostentatious. The bearing of the great military chieftain, even in the meridian of his glorious career, was always kind and considerate. With his military family, his dignified courtesy was often dashed with a lively humor, and a pleasant raillery, rather than severity of demeanor, sometimes, urged his young men on to greater zeal and watchfulness. He was always looking after his soldiers, organizing them; and as far as possible, providing for their necessities. Mrs. Lee and her family were setting an example to our Southern matrons by knitting socks and gloves, which she sent in batches to General Lee, who portioned them out to his suffering army. In one letter he wrote: "There were sixty-seven pairs of socks in the bag which I brought from Richmond with me yesterday. One dozen of the Stuart socks had double heels. Can't you teach Mildred that stitch?" Picture the great military commander, after a conference with the President, carefully carrying a bag of socks back to his army, knit by the fingers of his wife and daughters! Again he wrote: "Your note with the socks arrived last evening. I have sent them to the Stonewall Brigade; including this last parcel, I have sent to that brigade 263 pairs. Still there are about 140, whose homes are within the enemy's lines, and who are without socks. Tell the young women to work hard for the brave Stonewallers." And so, while he planned and fought, his wife and daughters like others of the Confederacy were plying their needles, night and day, to relieve the sufferings of the soldiers in the army. And as resolute and courageous as the men were, the mothers and daughters of the Confederacy were equal to them in fortitude, and in patient endurance of the sufferings and privations in the long protracted period of the war. Mourning and desolation came to every household, but the spirit of the women of the South was unconquerable.

Captain Ashe gave a succinct account of the great campaigns of the war, of Lee's unsurpassed generalship, and of the final disaster at Appomattox. We make room for a single quotation, the defeat of Grant at Cold Harbor:

Twelve days Grant spent in trying to drive Lee from Spottsylvania, and at last, weary of the effort, in sore disappointment, he solemnly withdraw at night and sought to make his way to the southeast, only to find that Lee had out-generaled him, and was still in his front at the North Anna. Not daring to attack Lee there, he again moved his army off. But Lee stood waiting for him at Cold Harbor.

At that time General Lee was ill in his tent. He had lost many valuable officers in the previous conflicts, and his organization was seriously impaired. Grant had now received reinforcements more in number than Lee's entire force, and General Lee was very apprehensive lest by sheer numbers Grant might break through his lines. His own ranks had, however, been strengthened by the fortunate arrival of two divisions; and General Hoke with his fresh troops occupied the position where the Federal army would make its chief assault; and when the serried columns of Federal brigades were hurled against Hoke's front, they were overwhelmingly repulsed. In one hour of terrific combat, on June 3rd, twelve thousand Federal soldiers lay stretched upon the field, and both officers and men recoiled from any further combat.

Twice the order was passed to renew the battle, but the Union soldiers did not move; the Federal army, twice the number of Lee's, sullenly refused to obey their orders and advance their flag against the Confederate lines. Thus ended in Federal disaster the pitched battles between Grant's vast hosts and the small Confederate army. Within one short month, in which the heaviest fighting known to history had taken place, Grant's immense army, after terrific losses, had failed to drive Lee from its path. As McDowell, McClellan, Pope, Burnside, Hooker and Meade had been withstood and their plans defeated, so now Grant's efforts had ended in his discomfiture. His movement "on to Richmond," from the north, was successfully blocked by the Confederate army.

Grant now found himself forced to resort to a different plan, and he crossed the James River. With his tremendous forces, he thought to extend his lines beyond the reasonable power of Lee to oppose him — that was his calculation. Still, Lee held his own against all odds, and the operations settled down to the siege of Petersburg, which lasted nearly a full year, during which Lee and his resolute Confederates were subjected to the most terrible vicissitudes in the annals of warfare.

The reserve power of the north now gave the Federal forces great advantages, and told with disastrous effect on the waning fortunes of the South. Sherman, with a great army, devastated Georgia and South Carolina, and

Grant's cavalry made the Valley of Virginia a scene of desolation.

At length the last gun was fired by Cox's Brigade, of Grimes' North Carolina Division, and the flag which the army of Northern Virginia had so often borne to victory, was furled forever.

Who can picture the poignant grief of Lee at such an ending of the terrific conflict; at such a termination of the great struggle the South had made to withstand the forces of the Union! The cause in which his country had embarked was lost! The cause for which tens of thousands had died, was no more.

His noble army; his flag emblazoned with glory, and the Confederacy, whose defense had been committed to his trust, had all passed away.

In those black hours of cruel fate, while yet in the agony of disappointment, and of grief and of love, and while the peans of his victorious foes rang in triumph throughout the continent, his lofty soul sent forth a note that only his great heart could have uttered: "Human fortitude should be equal to all human calamity."

Success generally bespeaks merit. Such success as was won by Stonewall Jackson and General Forrest is the highest proof of great merit. The victories of Lee will also attest to posterity his title to immortal fame, and the final disaster that overwhelmed him cannot detract from it. The adverse circumstances that at last surrounded the South rendered victory impossible. Lee did not inaugurate the war; he did not advise it; he deplored it. Its entire conduct was not in his keeping; he was given an army command, and he made it an army of heroes — the most glorious army in the annals of time.

The beleaguered, blockaded South, without military supplies, finally exhausted its resources. Its money became worthless, its provisions failed, suffering and privation and hunger pervaded the land. The great North, with its large population, its numerous factories, its extensive commerce, its immense wealth, had the world for its storehouse, and its supply of men, as well as of material, was almost inexhaustible. The Northern people pledged the world that in ninety days they would subjugate the South. Time after time they flashed the news through the courts of Europe that in ninety days they would crush the rebellion. Their ninety days grew to four long years. Many a gallant army they sent out with flying banners, singing "on to Richmond," only to be hurled back, defeated, beaten, routed, with colors trailing, and the North country mourning for the gallant spirits who had fallen beneath the heavy blows of Lee and his Southern heroes.

If to the South the war brought great sorrow and suffering and disaster, in like manner every hamlet at the North mourned for fallen sons. Billions of money were expended, and hundreds of thousands of lives were sacrificed in the effort to subjugate the Southern people.

Whatever were the motives, the influences that urged Northern statesmen to appeal to the sword, instead of resorting to peaceful methods, to the Northern people, their course proved a costly undertaking, even though it involved the South in utter ruin and desolation.

With the cessation of hostilities, General Lee, with that high conception of duty that had ever governed his conduct, set an example for the Southern people of accepting the situation and resolutely returning to the paths of peace. In four months after his flag was furled and his army was paroled, he entered upon new duties as president of Washington College at Lexington, Va., and his example as a citizen was as inspiring to the South as his military career had been glorious.

Duty, he had said, was the sublimest word in the English language, and he demonstrated by his refusal to lend his great name to commercial enterprises, which would have brought him wealth; that in his opinion wealth is a matter of secondary consideration, and that character and virtue are above all price. In peace, he was as admirable as in war; and his example as a noble, high-minded, Christian gentleman has had a refining influence in the homes of the Southland.

At last, in the autumn of 1870, he passed away, and was gathered to his fathers, leaving as a heritage to the Southern people the rich legacy of his immortal fame and of his pure, noble character.

In conclusion, let me quote from the autobiography of Lord Wolsely, his estimate of our beloved hero:

"General Lee was one of the few men who ever seriously impressed and awed me with their natural, their inherent greatness. Forty years have come and gone since our meeting, yet the majesty of his manly bearing, the genial, winning grace, the sweetness of his smile, and the impressive dignity of his old-fashioned style of address come back to me among the most cherished of my recollections. * * * * He spoke of the future with confidence — it was just after the battle of Antietam (Sharpsburg) — although one could clearly see he was of no very sanguine temperament.

"Even when the great and noble Christian captain referred to the bad treatment of Southern soldiers and people by the Yankees, he showed no resentment or bitterness, while deploring the fact. He even showed no resentment when he told of the destruction of his own home at Arlington Heights, near Washington, which his wife had inherited from General Washington.

"He had merely gone with his State, Virginia — the prevailing principle that had influenced most of the soldiers I spoke with during my visit to the South. He was, indeed, a beautiful character, and of him might truthfully be written, 'In righteousness he did judge and make war.'"

This tribute from England's famous military critic sustains our own view of Lee's greatness and character. His nature was not only lofty and noble, but his character was beautiful.

Such was the chief champion of the Southern people in their contest to maintain and preserve the independence won for by them by the blood and sacrifices of their Revolutionary Fathers. We honor him now, and posterity will venerate his name.

After centuries have rolled by — when all his contemporaries shall have passed into obscurity, the name of Lee, like that of Washington, will still be luminous with a lustre of glory, and his fame will be perpetuated as the noblest, the knightliest, and the most illustrious patriot who ever drew sword in his country's cause.

The Crosses of Honor

As the applause died away after the conclusion of the address, the band rendered *Tenting on the Old Camp Ground*, and then the audience, led by a cornet sang General Lee's favorite hymn *How Firm a Foundation*. Next was read by Adjutant Birdsong the rules and regulations governing the presentation of Crosses of Honor to Confederate veterans, and following this the following names were read as those to whom the Daughters of the Confederacy presented these at this time, the names being:

S. H. Black, Company G, Forty-ninth Regiment.
C. M. Busbee, Company E, Fifth Regiment.
W. D. Clanton, Company B, Thirteenth Regiment.
W. Gregory, Company E, Fifty-first Regiment.
E. B. Goelet, Company D, Tenth Regiment.
M. Hill, Company A, Eleventh Regiment.
H. Johnson, Company A, Fifty-third Regiment.
D. Owen, Company I, Nineteenth Regiment.
J. Pierce, Company H, Twenty-seventh Regiment.
J. A. Smith, Company C, Fifty-third Regiment.
W. A. Torrence, Company B, Twenty-eighth Regiment.
T. G. Williams, Company I, Thirty-third Regiment.
John M. Fleming, Company E, Gumstead Regiment, Ark.
J. G. B. Grimes, A. Q. M., Fourth North Carolina Regiment.
J. M. Goodwin, Company C, Forty-seventh North Carolina Regiment.

W. H. Lyon, Company I, Sixth North Carolina Regiment.
W. H. Mumford, Company D, Sixty-seventh North Carolina Regiment.

Of these there were present but Messrs. M. Hill, J. M. Fleming and W. H. Lyon. To receive the other Crosses, which went to veterans at the Home, Capt. R. H. Brooks, superintendent of the Soldiers' Home, was designated by the chapter, while relatives took those of kinsmen unavoidably absent. As the three veterans came forward there was applause for each, and more applause was heard as tiny granddaughters of the Confederacy pinned the crosses on the lapels of the coats of the men who had once faced the foe, the little ladies being Elizabeth Hill, Annie Lee Wynne, Mary Stronach and Lillian Riddick, all sweet little misses.

The Rear Guard

Mrs. F. A. Olds was next introduced, and she read most feelingly a poem, *The Rear Guard*, as follows:

The guns are hushed. On every field, once flowing
   With war's red flood, May's breath of peace is shed,
And spring's young grass and gracious flowers are growing
   Above the dead.

Ye gray old men whom we this day are greeting,
   Honor to you, honor and love and trust!
Brave to the brave! Your soldier hands are meeting
   Across their dust.

Bravely they fought who charged when flags were flying
   In cannon's crash, in screech and scream of shell;
Bravely they fell, who lay alone and dying
   In battle's hell.

Honor to them! For graves to-day are flinging
   Up through the soil peace-blooms to meet the sun.
And daisied heads to summer winds are singing
   Their long well done.

Our vanguard, they went with hot blood flushing,
   At battle's din, at joy of bugle's call.
They fell with smiles, the flood of young life gushing.
   Full brave the fall!

But braver yet, who when the war was ended,
   And bugle's call and wave of flag was done,

Could come back home, so long left undefended.
    Your cause unwon.

And twist the useless sword to hook of reaping.
    Rebuild the home, set back the empty chair.
And brave a land where waste and want were keeping
    Guard everywhere.

All this you did, your courage strong upon you.
    And out of ashes wreck, a new land 'rose.
Through years of war no braver battle won you.
    'Gainst fiercer foes.

And now to-day a prospered land is cheering
    And lifting up her voice in lusty pride
For you gray men, who fought and wrought, not fearing
    Battle's red tide.

Our rear guard ye, whose step is slowing, slowing;
    Whose ranks, earth-thinned, are filling otherwise;
Who wore the gray, the gray, alas! still showing
    On bleaching hair.

For forty years you've watched this land grow stronger,
    For forty years you've been its bulwark, stay;
Tarry a while; pause yet a little longer
    Upon the way.

And set our feet where there may be no turning,
    And set our faces straight on duty's track,
Where there may be for stray, strange gods no yearning,
    Nor looking back.

General Robert E. Lee — Captain Samuel A. Ashe

And when for you the last tattoo has sounded,
  And on death's silent field you've pitched your tent;
When, bowed through tears, the arc of life has rounded
    To full content,

We that are left will count it guerdon royal.
  Our heritage no years can take away;
That we were born of those, unflinching, loyal.
    Who wore the gray.

                     — Irene Fowler Brown
                             Memphis, Tenn.

    Applause greeted this, and as it ended Mrs. Olds again appeared. She said: I thank you all for that, but what I came back to say was that it had been agreed by the Daughters of the Confederacy that when *Dixie* was sung or played each veteran or daughter should arise, and in this I ask the audience to join. Then as *Dixie* was played by the band the audience stood while the loved music of the South swelled forth.
    This closed the events of the programme and the patriotic exercises were concluded with the benediction, delivered by Dr. M. M. Marshall, after which many of the audience waited to congratulate Captain Ashe, and to speak in words of love of that great soldier and chivalric gentleman, Robert E. Lee, for whom once again Raleigh had honored itself in honoring his memory.

About the Author

Captain Samuel A'Court Ashe is honored not only as a Confederate soldier, but also as a distinguished historian of the South. Samuel Ashe was born to William S. Ashe and Sarah Green on September 13, 1840, in New Hanover County, North Carolina. The Ashe family was prominent in the history of North Carolina since the state's earliest years. The original member of the family was from England. John Ashe came to this country in 1727. During the Revolutionary War, seven members of the Ashe family were officers, more than any other family in the state. Captain Ashe's great-grandfather was elected governor of North Carolina in 1795. His father was a representative in the US Congress before the War for Southern Independence.

Samuel Ashe entered the US Naval Academy at Annapolis in September of 1855. At that time only 15 students had graduated, but since the Academy started in 1851, its student body was small. Ashe left the Academy in 1858 because of constant sea sickness.

In 1861, when North Carolina seceded, Samuel Ashe entered service as an officer of the state of North Carolina. He was a lieutenant in the State Engineer and Artillery Corps engaged in putting the Cape Fear defenses in condition. He served briefly at the Charleston Arsenal where he tested the first bronze cannon cast in South Carolina.

Ashe was appointed by President Davis as a captain in the regular Confederate Army in June of 1862, and served as assistant adjutant general to General William Dorsey Pender where he participated in Pettigrew's Charge at the Battle of Gettysburg. He then served as

Captain Samuel A'Court Ashe

an ordnance officer at Battery Wagner on Morris Island, Charleston, SC. Next Ashe was transferred to the Fayetteville Arsenal where he served for the remainder of the War.

He served throughout the four years of the war and never officially surrendered to Union officials — a fact he was proud of in his later years. His war record was not unusual or outstanding. He served with devotion and to the satisfaction of his superiors. He holds the distinction of being the last surviving commissioned officer of the Confederate States Army having been commissioned by President Davis himself.

Captain Ashe excelled in his activities after the war. He took a prominent part in the reorganization and rebuilding of the North Carolina state government. He started his post-war career modestly. In 1866 "he felt fortunate to be a sleeping car conductor on the train running from Wilmington to West Point, GA." 1873 found him practicing law in Raleigh, being partners with Senator A. S. Merrimon and Judge Thomas Fuller. He served as chairman of the State Democratic Committee, a conservative in the General Assembly and was editor and owner of the Raleigh *News & Observer* for 14 years. During this time his writings had a wide influence across the state. At ninety years of age, he was still active as clerk of the US District Court in Raleigh. He was active in the United Confederate Veterans, serving for many years on the staff as a brigadier general. On the day before his death, he was elected an officer in the newly formed Military Order of the Stars and Bars at the annual Sons of Confederate Veterans reunion in Columbia, SC.

Samuel Ashe was an accomplished author. He edited the six volume *Biographical History of North Carolina* in 1905 – 1907. For years many of his articles were published in the *Confederate Veteran* magazine. At the time of its publishing, in 1908, his two volume *History of North Carolina* was commended by high authorities as the most complete history of any state ever published. A Mr. Emerton, in a review of this work, stated "It should be in every library, in every school, in every home. The state of North Carolina, the South, and the nation owe a debt to this painstaking and unusual scholar."

His most important work — *A Southern View of the Invasion of the Southern States and The War of 1861–65* was published in 1935. Think for a minute — Captain Ashe was born in 1840; in 1935, when he published his finest work he was 95 years old. In honor of his 98th birthday, a group of his friends published a second edition of this book as a present to him. He knew of this tribute and unfortunately passed away two weeks before his 98th birthday.

He never forgot his War experiences and always believed in the right of secession. He once said of Abraham Lincoln "one of the most terrible tyrants in history" and who "did more evil than any man known to the world."

Captain Ashe helped lead the movement to erect the Confederate Monument at the Capitol on Union Square in Raleigh with his newspaper columns. Captain Ashe has a memorial in his honor not far from the Confederate Monument. He died on August 31, 1938, and is buried in Oakwood Cemetery beside his wife, overlooking the Confederate Section. On the day of his death, the Confederate Flag flew at half-mast over the Capitol in Raleigh, an honor reserved for Confederate Memorial Day and General Lee's Birthday.

Other publications from

Lincoln As The South Should Know Him
.... O.W. Blacknall

Truth of the War Conspiracy of 1861
.... H. W. Johnstone

A Story Behind Every Stone
.... Charles E. Purser

As You May Never See Us Again
.... Joel Craig and Sharlene Baker

Additional Information and Amendments to the North Carolina Troops 1861 – 1865 Volume I & II
.... Charles E. Purser

Memoir of Nathaniel Macon of North Carolina
.... Weldon N. Edwards

More information available at
www.scuppernongpress.com

The Scuppernong Press
PO Box 1724
Wake Forest, NC 27588

www.ingramcontent.com/pod-product-compliance
Lightning Source LLC
Chambersburg PA
CBHW050547300426
44113CB00012B/2299